PRAISE FOR *HEADING HOME*

Poetry, humor, wisdom, g˙   *˙ading Home*. This book offers g   ˙, the natural world, small town   ˙ures best noticed and described b   ˙ural critic, part poet, part wande   ˙˙˙˙˙ guide, whether pondering the sorr   ˙˙, ˙˙e joys of the seasons, or the cultural eccentricities of the modern-day West. In the spirit of Thoreau, Dillard, and deBuys, this book took me on a thoughtful journey down roads of inquiry that deepened my own. I loved this book.

       —**Laura Pritchett**, author of *Stars Go Blue* and *Red Lightning*

Peter Anderson is gracefully gifted at demonstrating how life's most mundane occasions, lost on most of us, may loom vast in an awakened heart. Reexamining the roads he took years ago—influenced by Kerouac and straight shots of serendipity—Anderson concludes, "My travels are all round-trips these days, Jack. I've given up anywhere for somewhere." That "given up" does not signal surrender. And that "somewhere," that edge "where settled meets wild," is inhabited by quite a variety of characters, which he sketches with an exhilarating, understated compassion you'll soon find yourself sharing. Every page of this marvelous book includes some glimpse, some hint, some touch that makes me feel better about being alive.

       —**William Pitt Root,** poet, editor, author of *Strange Angels*

Peter Anderson's poetic sensibilities shine through language that is precise and efficient. In *Heading Home* he balances levity and humor with insight and wisdom. Reading through these pages, one feels they are on the road with Anderson, exploring the vast, beautiful, and empty corners of the American West. When I reached the end of this journey I wanted to start all over again. This is by far one of the best books I've read in a long time.

       —**Iver Arnegard, a**uthor of *Whip & Spur*, Associate Professor of Creative Writing at Colorado State University-Pueblo

"I've given up anywhere for somewhere," writes Peter Anderson, and it's our blessing that he did. Anderson is a listener, a watcher. With humor and curiosity, he guides us through some of Colorado's less-sung landscapes, leading us through the seasons, across the highways, and into the more ineffable journeys of aging, parenting, loss, and the rewards of committing to one place. I love this book.
—**Rosemerry Wahtola Trommer**, author of *Even Now: Poems and Drawings* and *The Less I Have: Poems*

Anderson is, and has always been, a prophet of place(s). The road, the night, the elements and the people he encounters all take communion at a table of memory, faith, hope, and loss. These essays have about them a writer's wit, a poet's eye and a good man's heart. They take us on journeys where you can feel the red dirt on your skin, hear the whoosh of passing big rigs, and hear the earth as it turns, mile upon mile toward our various human destinations. In *Heading Home* we find love and belonging after a life of searching.
—**aaron a. abeyta**, author of *colcha* and *Rise, Do Not Be Afraid*

HEADING HOME

HEADING HOME

HEADING HOME

Field Notes

PETER ANDERSON

CONUN
DRUM
PRESS

AN IMPRINT OF BOWER HOUSE

DENVER

Cover Art by Beatris Burgoin

Library of Congress Control Number: 2017936763

ISBN: 978-1-942280-21-7

10 9 8 7 6 5 4 3 2

" . . . *for everything which is natural*
which is infinite which is yes"

—e. e. cummings

CONTENTS

III. Habitation

IV. The Big Empty

I.

MOTHER ROAD

" . . . We had longer ways to go. But no matter, the road is life."

—Jack Kerouac

" . . . Beware, O wanderer, the road is walking too."

—Jim Harrison

LEAVING ST. ELMO

ONE-ROOM CABIN IN AN ABANDONED FALSE-FRONT TOWN, THE DIVIDE off to the west, mountains honeycombed with all the old diggings. One winter, the only resident, I read old newsprint, learned to see St. Elmo the way it once was, smelter smoke narrow-gauge high-grade dreams, before the paper dollar wrecked the gold and silver market and the railroad pulled out. My place, the only light for miles, threw its rays out toward the Milky Way. Woodstove, sleeping bag on the floor, cans of Del Monte Fruit, Campbell's Soup, Maxwell House Coffee, mice snapping traps in the cupboard. Outside, night winds blew prospecting ghosts down the mountain. If the lower elevations called me now and then, it was only until the nightmares came: visions of après ski tights and fur jackets wandering the newly fern-barred streets of this ghost town turned resort, or worse, the old cabin surrounded by an invasion of doublewides, riding the wave of some meth-headed oil and gas boom. When the mine at Climax shut down, it was the bust that finally got to me—storefronts boarded up from Leadville to Salida, down-valley friends leaving the country, nights darker than the shafts inside the mountain above town. The two-lane that ran south by southwest over Poncha Pass and Wolf Creek slid down the switchbacks on the sunset side promising brighter lights . . . *Durango, Durango* . . . and possibility. So I folded up the map of home I'd made and it was adiós old shack, adiós old town, and hello to a road I couldn't help but ride.

Night Ride in the
Red Desert

Remember when you were headed west out of Wamsutter, measuring the after-midnight miles with a half-emptied six-pack, and you had the hammer down and nothing but empty up ahead? Remember, somewhere west of Bitter Creek, you stopped for that rough-necked renegade leaning into the wind who told you he was so hungry, he could eat the ass off a skunk? Remember the eatum-up truck-stop neon blazing like Christmas with the voltage cranked and all those big buckets of bolts blowing diesel in the parking lot? Remember how your roughneck pal went silent over chicken-fried steak, and how you picked at a piece of pecan pie from the Pleistocene, and how the cat-eyed waitress called you *hon* and made it all okay? Remember dropping your new friend off at daybreak—Highway 189 north to Diamondville—and how he told you to keep the shiny side up and the greasy side down, and how you said *fer sure*, and how it was easier to believe, back then, that everyone was a good buddy just waiting to happen?

BACKBUMPER GOSPEL

AMERICA, I READ YOUR BACKBUMPER GOSPEL AND EVERY STATE CAN
preach it proud:

> Lone Star Lone Star, leave us alone Star. Sweet Home,
> Dairyland, the Canyon State. Sportsman's Paradise, Silver
> State pair-of-dice. Aviation Birthplace, First in Flight.

> Potatoes Potatoes, Famous Potatoes. Great Ocean Faces,
> Greatest Snow on Earth.

> Sunshine, Sunshine, Land of Enchantment. Evergreen
> Treasure, Ten Thousand Lakes.

> Green Mountain, Constitution, Land of Lincoln. Vaca-
> tionland, Volunteer, Live Free or Die.

America, you've got shine, but everyone knows you lay out a
long shadow too. I heard Jesus was driving a Mack and reading
your back and spinning the gospel through Oklahoma—Peace
Garden, Peace Garden, Show Me the Peace Garden. Aloha,
Aloha, The Last Frontier.

LETTER FROM THE
MOTHER ROAD

OLD ROUTE 66 ON THE EASTERN EDGE OF FLAGSTAFF. NEAR THE Great Wall Chinese Buffet, Bubba's Real Texas Barbecue, and the Purple Sage Motel (American-owned), we are sitting in the customer lounge of the Econolube. An oil change is rarely just an oil change for this old Dodge, with a big fender dent, a wandering eye of a right headlight, and 170 G's on the odometer. "All four tires are cuppin' real bad," says Calamity Jane, the service manager. "You're a blowout waiting to happen."

For the Navajo family waiting with us in the lounge—grandmother, mother, father, uncle, boy about five, girl about two, all of whom rode to town in a late model Silverado—the news isn't quite as dire. Only a frayed belt. "Oh, you might make it back to Tuba," says Calamity, "but it'll shred before summer." The father knows that when the belt goes, so does the AC. And there will be many family rides to Flag during the long hot summer on the rez. He gives Jane the nod. So do I. And we all enter Econolube limbo.

Now the mom watches over their little boy, who rolls a red rubber ball across the floor, while her little girl empties a Tupperware bowl of plastic cowboys and Indians. The grandma watches a French chef on a wall-mounted TV whipping up egg whites for a dessert called charlotte russe, which features a ring of brandy-soaked ladyfingers. "Mmmmm," she says. The uncle is working on a giant Slurpee from 7-Eleven. My daughter, reads *Harry Potter and the Sorcerer's Stone.* The Dad and I satisfy ourselves with back issues of *Field & Stream.*

The little boy's ball rolls my way again. I catch it, smile, and roll it back. The little girl tells her mom that the cowboys have won again. All her Indians lie in a heap around a plastic totem pole. The little boy rolls the ball and this time he and it go out the door and into the parking lot. The father puts down his *Field & Stream* and goes out to retrieve him. And when they return, the father brushes the dirt off the boy's bare feet. "You're startin' to look like one of them Blackfoot induns," he says.

Three hundred miles of road separate our place in the San Luis Valley from this family's home in Tuba City, but we live only a few miles north of a mountain they know as Tsisnaasjiní, sacred mountain of the east, and we know as Blanca, the one that still has snow. So, yes, we see each other from a distance and we name the world in different ways, but today in the Econolube, we laugh as neighbors, which the mountain knows we really are.

ESPRESSO IN KAYENTA

ROAD WEARY AFTER THE DRIVE UP FROM PAGE, I STOP IN KAYENTA, near a handmade espresso sign on a sheet of plywood, and I follow the arrows—*coffee this way*—hoping for a highly caffeinated oasis between fast-food joints. I walk through a gate, into a courtyard, and toward the door in an old stucco building. *Try a cool, refreshing Nava-Joe*, says another sign and I let it reel me into the Blue Shepherd Coffee Shop. "Does that Nava-Joe pack a pretty strong buzz?" I ask the young barista. "Four shots," he tells me, which sounds about right for the drive ahead.

As he's fixing my drink, I notice an open Bible on the counter and ask if he's been reading scripture. "Ezekiel 37:9," he says, and then he offers the Word itself: *"Come from the four winds, O breath, and breathe on these slain, that they may come to life. That's what He did . . . my mother and father were dead to the bottle. He brought them back to life. Happens all the time at my church."

He hands me my Nava-joe and asks me where I'm from and I say Colorado . . . San Luis Valley. He asks me where I've been and I tell him I've been driving a big circle—Colorado through red-rock country, home along the Arizona Strip, now across the rez to the San Juans. I am reminded of a man whose home I will pass along the way. "I knew a circuit-riding Navajo preacher who loved the gospels *and* the old ways," I say. "Is your faith like that?"

8

"No," he says. "I don't worship all the spirits I grew up with. I go to the one who created it all. That's why I call this place the Blue Shepherd. My people are sheepherders . . . my savior is the Shepard." Then we are quiet for a while. Outside, a gusting spring wind.

I ask him if more people are coming through now that winter is waning. "Yeah, mostly Europeans. French, Italians, Germans . . . No Japanese, though . . . they're tea drinkers," he says and for the first time in our conversation, he cracks a smile. "I'm Kyle, by the way." We shake hands, talk a while longer, and then it's time to get going. "Stop by if you're back through again," he says. I say I will.

A few miles out of Kayenta, heading northeast to Four Corners, a dust devil whirls up from the south, leaving a thin film of red sand on the windshield. I could wash it all away, but it softens the bright light, so I let it be—this remnant of the wind made visible.

RODEO WEEKEND, DUCHESNE, UTAH

DEAR SPARKY,

On this Saturday morning, it's easy to fall in love with this town. You've seen this same rodeo parade in Cortez—sequin-dressed cheerleaders and snare-drum drill teams, Model T's, an old cowboy on a stud bull named Louie whose horns are capped with silver. The rodeo queen smiles and waves as if cleaning the air with Windex; firemen shoot hoses at sunbaked kids who run beside their red truck; Miss Little Ute does sign language to a scratchy record about a young Indian boy going off to war. E-Z Auto Parts boys pretend to fix a demo derby jalopy; Skunky's Sanitation has an outhouse disguised as a rocket ship. Young moms and their blonde-haired newborns—the latest crop of Latter Day Saints-to-be—ride by on a flatbed trailer.

Later, I give my ticket to an attendant whose arms are covered with spaceship tattoos, then ride the Rock-O-Plane, raining spare change on the pavement below. In the rodeo stands, I hesitate before doffing my hat for the national anthem and the flag that we have just wrapped around another war.

Later, the rodeo clown struts through the arena. "Couldn't get to sleep last night," he says.

"How come?" asks the rodeo announcer.

"Someone kept eating candy bars in the next room."

"Candy bars?"

"Yeah, they kept shouting, 'O Henry O Henry!'"

For a while, I forget my unease or try to. Later, out on Highway 40, lightning splits the Uinta Basin sky like shock-and-awe Scuds over Baghdad. How good it would be to sit with you in silence at the meeting house. No matter what the road atlas says, I am a long way from home.

Puttin' on the Ritz at the Little Bighorn

It is not the tune one would expect to hear near a meadow known for its dead. But a Sioux jazzman named Smoke has already played "Garryowen," the song that bolstered Custer and his men as they rode into Medicine Tail Coulee. And he has finished blowing "Taps" for all the fallen along the Little Bighorn.

Now, risen from the commemorative battlefield on Kennard Real Bird's ranch, local Crow horsemen, who just rode as the Sioux, and some U.S. Cavalry buffs from Michigan who rode as Custer and the 7th, trailer their bays and pintos. Behind the emptied grandstand and beside the fry-bread booth holding out for one last sale, Smoke blows a familiar riff: *Dah, Dah, Dah, dadada, Dah, Dah, Dah, dadada, Dah, Dah, Dah . . . dadadadadada*

Later, I drive through the gray rain along the Greasy Grass, humming his jubilee tune and conjuring a scene way off Broadway: powwow prancer Irving Berlin—stone in one ear and lightning bolts painted on both cheeks—shakes his tail feathers, Crazy Horse sashays across the meadow in high hat and white spats, and a chorus line of Sioux warriors ride by in perfectly syncopated dressage, all of them doing their Little Bighorn fancy dance and puttin' on the Ritz.

SUMMER CROSSING

OUT ON THE NIGHT ROAD THROUGH KANSAS, WITH GARCIA'S GUITAR leads winging like barn swallows around the eaves of old-but-good *American Beauty* tunes, lightning flashed around the hole in a prairie storm. I thought I would drive into Missouri under that circle of stars, but the clouds bellied over and sheets of rain washed over the wipers, streaking the red left behind by truck-trailer taillights and bending the white beams cast by an improbable electric cross. Just past the cross, I drove by a lone exit sign. "Vespers," it said. I imagined white-cowled Trappists, the lit cross spilling light into an otherwise dark chapel, wind whistling through the mesh of window screens and into their psalms. "If I knew the way, I would take you home," Garcia sang, as the last of the white light rippled in the rearview, and lay down behind the prairie rising.

DEEP CALLS TO DEEP

END-OF-DAY DRIVE WEST OF GUNNISON, A PERFECT ROUND SUN behind the sky's memory of wind and sand. See the truck, small as a toy out at peninsula's end, and farther out, the man, only a dark speck at the far edge of lake-rim thaw. Has he heard how the ice broke up yesterday and stranded two fishermen from Denver? Does he listen now for the first hint of fracture, or is he lost in the depths where his silver spinner flickers past the big browns so lean and slow this time of year? Maybe it will draw them from their torpor, they will give chase, and he will feel again the pulse he cannot see, which passes as fast as his own, just enough to invite another cast, and another, into the last light . . . this man out fishing on the edge of the ice.

LETTER TO JACK KEROUAC
AFTER REREADING
ON THE ROAD

*"Whither goest thou, America, in thy shiny car
in the night?"*

—Jack Kerouac

DEAR JACK,

America's car is less shiny these days and more like the bald-tired, rusting-fendered Dodge I drive. Out on the night road for the holidays, with two young daughters and my wife of twenty years, I've been thinking about you and how things have changed.

"What's your road, man?—holyboy road, madman road, rainbow road, guppy road, any road. It's an anywhere road for anybody anyhow," you once wrote. For me, it's a dad's road now, Jack. You used to poke fun at middle-aged guys like me: "They have worries, they're counting the miles, they're thinking about where to sleep tonight, how much money for gas, the weather . . ." And I admit, I am thinking about all those things more than I used to as we head north to Idaho for a visit with the northwestern contingent of my clan.

"What is that feeling when you're driving away from people and they recede on the plain till you see their specks dispersing?" you asked us. "It's the too-huge world vaulting us, and it's good-by," you said, "but we lean forward to the next crazy venture beneath the skies." Well, for me, those crazy ventures are done. I will never again ride in a Volkswagen bug with two other young guys on a highway in South Dakota and encounter the too-good-to-be-true roadside attraction of four hitchhiking girls from the Sioux reservation westbound for Hollywood. I will never ride again in that bug with six other wayfarers and accompanying packs, one of which contains a big bag of hemp-quality wild reefer harvested on those same Great Plains. As you know, Jack, that's a young man's game.

Tonight, we will roll west across the "rooftop of America" and beyond onto the Colorado Plateau, past the intricate red-rock folds and fissures of the San Rafael Swell, across the formidable Wasatch Range, and into the Salt Lake City night where the Angel of Moroni is still shining atop the Mormon temple, further north onto the Snake River plains of southern Idaho where a mobile home, all by itself, somewhere out in the vast lava lands on the cut off between Minidoka and Shoshone, bravely shines its Christmas lights into the same great American night that you loved to write about.

But the road is different now. It doesn't go everywhere like it used to. Sometimes I envy my freewheeling friends for whom any destination is still possible. But for me, it is no longer true, as you once suggested, "that nothing [is] behind me, everything [is] ahead of me, as is ever so on the road." Some time ago, I drove past the sign that says there is more in the rearview than I will ever see through the windshield. Since then I've chosen a partner and a home, and these days I'm watching my two girls climbing rocks on the western flanks of the Sangre de Cristos. My travels are all round-trips these days, Jack. I've given up anywhere for somewhere, which strikes me now as a fair trade.

II.

NIGHTLIFE

" . . . great sleep of blue; reach far within me; open doors . . ."

—William Stafford

MIDDLE AGE

LATE NIGHT IN LARAMIE. THE WHISTLE OF A WESTBOUND FREIGHT
train lingers in the sultry summer air. Translucent drapes across
a wide-open window rarely move. Even one sheet feels heavy
on you. The black dog on the floor stretches and sighs. A loiter-
ing moon throws its light across your bed.

So you surrender to the big moon and get up. And you let the
black dog into the passenger seat of the Chevy and drive down
Fremont. You bang a right onto 3rd Street, and drive the post-
closing-time main drag down to Clark, where you turn left and
cross the bridge over the freight yards, imagining some drifter,
bedded down in the dark corner of a boxcar below, hoping for
some shut-eye and a free ride to Rock Springs.

South by southwest on Highway 130, with the lights of Laramie disappearing in the rearview, you look out toward the great
moonlit arc of a high ridge in the distance. Medicine Bow. And
you ride the rising plains past a café and a white church and into
the lodgepole foothills where Swedish tie hacks once cut pines
for the westering tracks of the Union Pacific. And you let the
road take you higher still, into the spruce and fir, until the forest
opens out at the base of the mountain.

On the trail above the lake, the black dog is a shadow except for his teeth and the whites of his eyes as he turns the switchback ahead of you. You follow him up through the talus on the ridge where the moon is so bright you can almost tell the color of the lichens on the big boulders up ahead. As you top out, you see the snowy ridges of the Never Summer Range lit up off to the south. On this clear Wyoming night, even humble towns like Laramie behind you, and Rawlins many miles off to the west, can dazzle you with light and seduce you from a distance.

On the summit, the black dog walks in a circle and lies down in the middle of it. You follow his lead, plant your feet on hard ground and your butt on a flat rock, and take in the old light of long-gone stars, fewer now in a full moon sky, but dizzying nonetheless. And you sit with the mountain, and everything above, below, before, and behind it, and rest in the center of a very big space.

On the way down, that space seems smaller as first light bends like a bow over the horizon, flaring the edges of a lingering cloud. But the moon is still perched over the mountain behind you. And it casts your shadow, impossibly large, across the switchbacks below. And then the sun rises up over the lip of the High Plains, and throws a second shadow back up the slope above you. And if the mountain was the center, you stand now in the middle: between the east where you came from and the west where all the light goes down.

THE RANGER AND
THE PORCUPINE

THEY ARE BOTH SOLITARY CREATURES WHO WANT TO BE LEFT ALONE.

The ranger has been swinging a Pulaski all day, clearing dead-fall off highline trails—fifteen miles and twenty lodgepole taken out. Back at the cabin he eats mac and cheese, burrows into his bag, and reads Abbey by kerosene until his lantern flares out.

The porcupine wants salt and knows where to find it. He crawls under the ranger's floor and gnaws and gnaws and gnaws on the plywood, loud as a bad memory, until the ranger can't stand it any longer. A million stars witness him in his Skivvies as he flashes a beam under the cabin and side-arms rocks which throw sparks when they hit the old stovepipe that is stashed there. Close may be good enough, he thinks. He goes back to bed, but the gnawing resumes.

Back into the night, he is armed, this time, with the assembled poles of a bivouac tent, which he wields like a pool cue. The porcupine huddles under the far corner of the cabin floor, but the ranger still lands a direct hit on the quill pig's snout, which, for a moment, he regrets. Then he remembers his dog's tongue hammered with quills. Somewhere a one-eyed coyote hunts only on his good side.

Finally they part ways, he hopes, as his nemesis waddles off into the dark spruce. The ranger crawls back into his cocoon where he drifts off into a vision of elk on a night ridge, echoing the bugling in the meadow below his camp. Meantime, the porcupine finds a pack saddle cinch, perfectly salted with horse sweat.

They are both solitary creatures who want to be left alone.

What the Old
Forester Told Me

—for Jack

SNOW CAME EARLY THAT YEAR. HAD A KID NAMED JACKSON CRUISING timber on the mountain and it was time to pack him out. Sky was full of mare's tails—another front coming in. I made good miles through the high spruce. Post-holing hip-deep snow on the way down, I saw something up ahead—a black sheep, left behind from the summer graze. It was stuck in a snowdrift . . . the harder it tried to get out, the deeper it dug in. I couldn't leave it like that, so I took out my .38 and put it down. And then I waited. And waited some more for Jackson who was lagging behind under a heavy load. Finally, he caught up. Said he'd had enough and wanted to lie down in the snow. "See that sheep?" I said, putting a hand on my holster. "I'm not leaving you here to freeze, either." Well, he kept up after that. When we made the last switchback, it was dark on the mountain, but the lights of town below us sure did shine.

Evening Along
the San Juan

We walk home from Cow Springs Trading Post where, over
dinner, you gave me Navajo words. *Shonto* means light playing
on the water, you said. *Iyonoshne* means I love you.

Iyonoshne . . . I can say it in another tongue as we walk the back
streets of Bluff, passing those old redstone homes. A woman in a
window pulls down her shade. Ten o'clock: Mormon midnight.
Nearing the bridge that crosses the sandy wash, we can see the
light blinking at the Mokee Motel . . . Mokee Motel . . . on the
western edge of town.

Beyond, the river carries a sliver of moon through some long-
gone dunes now homed in stone, past *mokee* steps and square
shouldered *kachinas*, past a white horse on a red slope of broken
shale, past morning primrose and skyrocket gilia, and on toward
Mexican Hat and the Goosenecks.

How does the river know when to leave a long meander for a
new channel? Hands joined as they were on that last river night
under the big cottonwood, we are crossing the dark bridge now.
And I wonder if my feet will find the ground.

CHRISTMAS IN
YELLOWSTONE

OUT PAST THE TOWN WHERE THE GAS HAZE HOVERED, PAST THE LAST
of the Polaris and Arctic Cat crowds, past the Canada geese
floating the black waters of the Madison and the snow-faced elk
pawing for grass along its banks, past the bleak trunks of the
lodgepole pine scorched during the fire of 1988, past the fuma-
roles and craters where bubbles sizzled over red-stained rock,
past coyote bones on the bottom of a deep steaming pool, past
the sign that says learn to love the unpredictable, past the geyser
where the little old lady once asked the ranger when the erec-
tion would happen, and not far from the thundering falls of the
Yellowstone, was their base camp—a half-dozen yurts humped
like a herd of bison beside a big canvas cook tent.

After pancakes and maple syrup and coffee and refills, after scrap-
ing off the old wax and corking in a new layer of green for
the early morning kick-and-glide through aspen scarred by the
paws of some now-sleeping griz and bent low under a recent
snow, after the ascent up the ridge of Mount Washburn in an
icy fog, after the lunch of ham sandwiches, Wheat Thins, and
ginger snaps, and Ardin describing the view of Hayden Valley,
the Absarokas, and Yellowstone Lake (which they could only
imagine), after the descent carving wide S-turns through a thin

crust over soft powder in the shadowless white light that hid all the contours, after the deadfall bushwack on the way home, after Christmas turkey in the cook tent and the reference librarian from Bozeman saying he was as full as a tick on a hypertensive dog, they marveled at the hoarfrost crystals silvered in headlamp light on the way back to the yurt.

Inside and warm, he lit the kerosene lantern and read out loud from Merton. And then they sat and centered, wrapped in sleeping bags, and listened to the wind and then nothing at all. And when they opened their eyes, she said, *How strong are your monkish vows anyway?* And he said, *I don't know, tempt me.* And she did. And later, he turned down the lantern and his long body curved around hers, and they watched the last of the blue flame fade.

LETTER TO THE OLD
MAN TWO YEARS GONE

I STILL SING *LIKE A DIAMOND IN THE SKY* WITH CAROLINE WHO USED
to wonder where you'd gone. She barely knew you. You barely
knew her. After the stroke it was a good day if you could remember her name. If she sees a blinking star, I tell her it might be you.
It might also be me, on a balcony this side of Orion, savoring
the glow of a smoke on the sly. Remember? Watching the night
planes, your smoke never reaching the light they leave behind,
and the falling stars that never quite find the ground.

There is still so much sky between us.

MEMORY LOSS

HIS MEMORY IS A MISMANAGED LIBRARY. THE SHELVER LIVES IN A
storage room, where he burrows through piles of books, some
of which were returned years ago. He has been daydreaming
about bonfires of paperbacks and has been seen drinking heavily
after work. The librarian worries about all the holes in the stacks.

Three things he was intent on remembering this morning:

  1.

  2.

  3.

He has bags under his eyes again. He can't keep up with all the
details he wants to record from his day. Already, he has forgotten the fireflies he saw the night before. When he dreams, he
pours more tea into full teacups.

He thought his poet friends were calling him Father Owl, as
in a dweller of the late night who dispenses occasional bits
of wisdom. But really, they were calling him Father Al, as in
Alzheimer's.

He once found his father in the hospital room, looking for his
"nozzer," which meant "wallet" in the old man's post-stroke
lingo.

Nozzer. Nozzer. Nozzer. Nozzer.
Car keys. Glasses. Wallet, wallet. Car keys.

He worries that if he takes an afternoon nap in the Mojave Motel, he will wake and not know where he is . . . where he is . . . where he is. . . . And even then, he will not know where he is.

OH, NICO

SUCCUBUS FROM THE TOBACCO LEAF, SOMETIMES I WISH YOU WOULD turn me loose but you have your ways and you know where to find me, usually at night on some mountain-town sidewalk after a few beers. You know how to get my attention, like the older but attractive woman stealing a French fry from my plate at the bar and grill. You love to flaunt yourself. And I am all too willing to entertain your flauntings. Oh, Nico. You are like the Harley-leathered bartender in that downtown Montrose tavern, one of the few places where they still let you in. Like her, you are both attractive and dangerous, and maybe that's the appeal. Or maybe it's how you leave me with my thoughts as I breathe you in. How you dance your night-sky tango when I let you go. It's true, I love to undo your slinky belt and slide off your see-through negligee. And you smell so good when you are naked and ready to burn. And I love the anticipation of lighting you up. And how you disappear and drift away saying *I'm here and I'm gone but there's more where that came from.* You drive me to drink when you do that, but then I want you even more. And you are always willing to come back. Damn you. Too often your scent lingers and it is clear that I have been with you. My wife hates you and so do my daughters. You took my old man. I hate you in the morning when you linger uninvited, though you can be pleasant over coffee. Leave now and don't come back. But you will and you will and you will. And I will say good-bye, good-bye, and good-bye. For now.

GRINGO'S LINGO FOR
A NIGHT ON THE TOWN

(found in *Lonely Planet Latin American Spanish
Phrasebook & Dictionary*)

Para mí, una copa de tequila.
I'll have a tequila.

Otra de la misma.
Same again, please.

¿Qué quieres tomar?
What would you like?

Es mi ronda. La próxima la pagas tú.
It's my round. You can get the next one.

Está pasando bien.
This is hitting the spot.

¿Cuál es tu signo del horóscopo?
What sign are you?

Tienes una personalidad preciosa.
You have a beautiful personality.

Me siento fenomenal.
I feel fantastic.

Te quiero muchísimo.
I really, really love you.

¿Dónde está el baño?
Where is the toilet?

Creo que he tomado demasiado. ¿Me puedes pedir un taxi?
I think I have had one too many. Can you call me a taxi?

GREAT DIVIDE
LONELY HEARTS CLUB

1. ME, RECENTLY RELOCATED INVESTMENT QUEEN, 55, BIG CITY SUC-
cessful and small-town bored, missing summers in Southampton.
Finding some solace in mountain sunsets and well-watered lawns.
Looking for bullish stock buddy ready for bottom fishing adven-
tures. You, strong jawed CEO look, Ivy League pedigree, with
a passion for cocktails, steaks, and the Dow, and a robust and
well-diversified portfolio. Country club experience preferred—
must know how to handle your putter. I'm eager to massage
your bottom line and watch your portfolio grow. Let's make
something happen before the closing bell. Please no democrats.
                                            —*Tiffy, Aspen, Colorado*

2. MILDLY DEPRESSED RIVER DUDE, 25, WITH LOW-WATER-BAD-BIZ
blues. I'm over the daily slog on this bony ass river, tired of
rubber and glue warehouse scene. Tip stash spent on 50-cent
PBRs at the Vic. Looking for shoulder-season sweetheart. Saving
for flight to Chile in November so your generous pocketbook a
plus. I'm tan, ripped, and ready for good-time float. Let's find a
way to ride out these lame riffles, baby. Late summer spark and
groove guaranteed, no commitments either way.
                                            —*Rip Raft, Salida*

3. POTATO FARMER, 57, BUSY WITH 450 ACRES OF RUSSETS, FINGER-lings, Rose Reds, and Purple Majesties, dizzy from too many years of riding the big circles. Looking for a woman, John Deere steady, who can straighten me out. Bulk truck driving skills a plus. Come waltz me through this harvest. If you'll bake, boil, mash, and hash, I'll oil up the skillet and wash the dishes.

—*Hollow Heart, Mosca*

4. HARDROCK MINER, 45, TOO-LONG SOLITARY MUCKER, WANTS DOU-ble-jacking gal with a steady hand. Hold that steel, and I'll ride the big sledge home. Let's take it down and make some hole together. Your hankering for rock dust, Silver Dollar closing time, a must. Me? All boom, no bust.

—*Buck, Leadville*

5. DISCOURAGED FEMALE EARTHLING, LOOKING FOR EXTRATERRES-trial with holographic or multidimensional transportation who can navigate Armageddon. I want a hunka-hunka cosmic cool who can unbind my consciousness and take me away. I'm no newbie on this circuit, so I know my intergalactic protocol. You want integrated cosmic awareness of space, time, and matter? I've got it down. Also handy with lasers and electromagnetic sig-nals. I'm waiting. Please don't leave me in the void much longer.

—*Astrid, somewhere near Highway 17, San Luis Valley*

TRUE NEWS FROM A SMALL-TOWN BEAT

"GIVE ME ALL THE MONEY IN YOUR CASH REGISTER," HE SAID.

"Are you serious?" asked the Loaf 'N Jug night-shifter.

"Yes," the old man said.

"Who do you think you are?"

"Well, I never done *this* before . . . how much you got in your register, anyway?"

"Not much," she said.

"Could you give me twenty dollars?"

"No, I can't."

"Howbout five?"

"No."

"Well, howbout a pack of smokes?"

"I'll give you a couple," she said.

"Bless you," he said.

"He was desperate," she would say later on.

Police are investigating.

WAKE AT THE SILVER CREST SALOON

DAMMIT, BOB, WHY DIDN'T YOU CHECK IN BEFORE YOU CHECKED OUT? Never mind, I know, your dark courage was too fragile for that.

The day after they found you, we gathered in Edgetown's only bar. All our pickers played that night. I thought of the way you would flash up and down the neck of your Martin like it was greased up and ready to light on fire. When you first got here, you said you were home. In this town full of misfits we hear that often. Many find a welcome at the end of the road they have not found elsewhere. Some of them even stay. But around here, the wind finds the cracks in your caulking. And where the wind travels, it leaves its holes, like the great rock arch beyond Penitente Canyon.

Now and then, I look up at your photo behind the bar, maybe raise a glass to your jukebox song. Occasionally, a newcomer notices the dates—1962-2006—and wonders what became of you. I tell them the wind shook your window one night and you decided to ride it home.

BATS

YOU LOOK DOWN INTO THE SHAFT OF AN ABANDONED IRON MINE, A dark mountain portal into a deep cavern. Your vision takes you only partway to the source of a slight breeze. Waiting for the bats is like dwelling in the borderlands between waking and sleeping. How long, how long? Then a deep stirring and the early thread of the dream appears. Only a few bats, thousands more will follow, riding this mountain tide into a world where you are a stranger. You know they listen to echoes that you can't hear. You admire their pirouettes as they emerge. Here, in the foothill twilight, what matters is the way they rise into a vast, whirling column. What matters is the breeze and the sound, like moving water, they leave in their wake. What matters is this great river of wings that ends as it begins. In darkness. Now you know where the night comes from.

FIREFLIES

I LEARNED A LONG TIME AGO THAT YOUR LIGHT WOULDN'T LAST TILL morning. I know now that your scientific name is *Lampyridae*, that the organ on your abdomen secretes your light, that you flicker for mates, sometimes for prey, that some of you eat only pollens and nectars, that some of you follow slime trails left by slugs which you eat with your long, grooved mandibles, that you must avoid frogs who gorge on you till they glow, that sometimes, say in the Great Smoky Mountains or in the jungles of Malaysia, you gather in great swarms and flash your lights in sync.

We have satellites that sweep across the sky—in sync with a super clock in Boulder, accurate to a millionth of a second—which help us aim our missiles. And we have many earthbound lights . . . lit cigarettes trailing home from the bars at closing time, pickups throwing their high beams down dark county roads, the flicker of prairie towns seen from airplane windows.

We are here, they all say.

And you're on your own, the night says back.

III.

HABITATION

"Wherever we looked the land would hold us up."

—William Stafford

WHERE I LIVE

I LIVE ON THE OUTSKIRTS OF AN END-OF-THE-ROAD TOWN, IN WHAT was once an old Spanish land grant, then a big spread of a ranch, now a subdivision where settled meets wild. I live just east of a creekside riparian zone, on the high end of the piñon-juniper and the low end of ponderosa, on the eastern edge of the San Luis Valley and the western flanks of the Sangre de Cristo Mountains in southern Colorado. I live on a threshold where roads end and trails begin, where the horizontal meets the vertical, where rain turns into snow.

If I know anything about being deeply at home, about *querencia*, I know it here where the wind curls up and away as it meets the mountain after crossing a valley the size of Connecticut. Sangre de Cristo. Blood of Christ. If it weren't for you, I'd blow eastward across the Great Plains. County Road T led me to this dead end where the only east is steep. The mountain helps me stay.

If Highway 17 is the river, this place is a way-back eddy that draws in the swimmers who aren't going anywhere in a hurry, who like to spin round in the current below the big rocks. We don't want to swim that fast anymore. Some of us look for sustenance in the still water . . . maybe we find it, maybe we don't. Some of us spin in and out again onto the highway that got us here. And some of us get stuck, turning round and round, wondering why we have come, watching the faster currents elsewhere moving, moving, moving.

We want slow and we don't. Post-retreat Buddhists mourn their departure, but like getting back to faster water. Locals seek out diversions from the same old same old, obsessing about apocalypse, predicting some Aquarian Mayan shift in the status quo, or just rolling up another reefer, spinning, spinning, spinning, and who the hell cares? Maybe it's true that we're all here because we're not all there.

But any river needs its eddies and eddy dwellers. We know that "fast" can take us down, so we have come to a town without traffic lights. Sometimes we venture back out into the mainstream like St. Francis leaving his cave. Some travel further than others. I can make it to Alamosa twice a week. Sometimes I envy those who go farther and faster. I read about them in alumni magazines before I toss them in the round file.

Where I live, the center is closer to the edge.

Skating the Rio
(January)

Other than a blue hole off to the west, from which a late afternoon sun throws a promised-land glow over the hills south of Del Norte, we are driving under a woolen-gray January sky. Crossing over the Rio Grande, gusts of Wolf Creek wind carry billowing sheets of snow down the frozen river toward the ranch where my daughter and I are headed.

Several miles east of Del Norte, we turn off the highway and follow the signs—old-fashioned white figure skates dangling from fence posts and pasture gates—to the river. There we find several people standing around a fire, a little girl roasting a marshmallow, someone cooking brats and chili on a nearby grill, an assortment of grown-ups and kids skating between two homemade hockey goals, and a pack of ranch dogs circling the commotion and chasing the puck, all of this out on a shoveled-off rink of Rio Grande river ice.

Pond hockey—river hockey here—gets in your blood. It has been in mine for a long time. And now as I sit down on a log bench to lace up my blades, and I hear skates carving up the ice and sticks slapping pucks, I remember a frozen scene some forty-five years ago: long strong striding with a good pal into the great beyond of a glassy black-iced lake, sliding the puck back and forth across the smoothness of it all, faster and farther, faster and farther, world without end, amen.

I could live in that flashback, but duty calls and I help my daughter lace up her skates. I grab her a short stick and show her how to lean on it for balance. She's a little wobbly, but she'll do fine. So I grab myself a stick out of the pile and soon we are out in the fray. And it's slapstick, slapstick, and poke away the puck. And it's weave left, weave right, and steer through a maze of long legs and short legs. I forget, for a short while, that I am now 57 and out of shape.

This ice, this freeze, unlike the Zambonied surface most skaters are used to, has its own topography—bumps, ripples, crisscrossing fissures, mushy edges. I relearn this when I get the puck on a fast break, catch a blade in a soft spot, and fly face first into a snowbank. "Yeah, it's a little soft over there," someone says.

All too soon, the sun has gone down. By now our silhouetted herd of puck-chasers has thinned out and we part ways even more to let the little skaters make some memories. My daughter gets the puck and slaps and whiffs and slaps and whiffs and then shoots again. Score!!

I will learn on the drive home that this game is now in her blood, too. Yes, I tell her, we will play again soon.

Mountain Time
(February)

Imagine this beginning: a molecule rides in your own exhale, water in the form of vapor, rising in a warmer stream of air to meet the cooler floor of a cloud, a cloud that the prevailing wind has nudged up against the western slope of a nearby mountain. Inside of the cloud, let's say this molecule, once a part of your own being, bumps into a grain of a grain of a grain of sand. And let's say some other water molecules mingling nearby drift into that same particle. Pretty soon, all those molecules, including your own, are linking up like star-to-the-right square dancers on a Saturday night.

Out in the valley, a trucker sits next to a window at Deb's Roadside Café. He clears a circle of vapor, his own breath in part, to look out the window. Clouds are piling up on the mountain. The good news: he's headed over the lowest pass headed out of the valley. The bad news: the curves are always in the shadows up there. "I hate hauling when it gets slick," he says to the waitress. "What kind of pie d'ya say you had?"

On a spread just north of town, a rancher in a flatbed rattles out over a frozen brown pasture hauling hay. He takes a pull off a Camel and blows out a puff of blue smoke while he listens to the snow advisory on the radio. Bring it on, he says to himself.

Then he recalls snowdrifts over fences and his whole herd spread out from hell to breakfast down County Road T.

Back on the slope of the mountain, the snow is falling. You see a doe nudging her two fawns toward the shelter of a piñon. Is it the windchill of the gust that just caught you head-on or is the temperature falling fast? You find the answer on the black sleeve of your wool shirt. What fell as pellets of hail only a few minutes ago now fall in the form of six-winged lattices, lovely translucent crystals. And they linger for as long it takes your exhaled breath to disappear.

Letter from the Side of the Mountain (March)

Dear Matt,

Sorry I missed your wedding. The East Coast seems farther away than it used to. And I'm sorry I haven't met your honey. Now your little boy is two, maybe three, and soon you will be driving him to school. When you were here, I was carrying Rosalea up the trail.

She is twelve now, Caroline is seven, and we are still here on the side of the mountain. If it weren't for a stop sign and a slight rise in the grade once we get down to the valley floor, I could almost roll the girls out to school in neutral. They humor me on our morning rides when I play them my classics—no, not make-em-smart-Mozart, but Jimi Hendrix, "Electric Ladyland," 1968.

Today, in the intro to "Gypsy Eyes," Mitch Mitchell is laying down his base-drum, top-hat groove—*boomchazz, boomchazz, boomchazz, boomchazz*. Jimi slides down the neck of his Stratocaster as we lose altitude. It's almost three hundred feet down to the flats. Sometimes that means moving out of cloud into clear, sometimes out of clear into cloud. Today light rays bend through the layers of our winter inversion and San Antonio Mountain appears to hover above the ground some 100 miles to the south.

Out on the valley floor, after we hit the county road straightaway, an elk herd morphs like mercury, one way then another, until a big cow takes the lead and turns them west. Then a raven swoops down in front of us and wings away with fresh roadkill. Meanwhile, Rosalea rides shotgun, covering Jimi's riff on her air guitar—*jiggajiggabingbingchackalack*—while Caroline covers the backbeat in the backseat—*boomchazz, boomchazz, boomchazz, boomchazz.*

We pass the wind-shagged whole-earth flag and come to a stop in the charter school parking lot. Some other parents and kids glance over our way and all of a sudden I feel very loud. *Jiggajiggabingbingchackalack.* I turn Jimi down. We unload and hug. And the girls walk off with their Scooby Doo lunchboxes toward the windswept double-wides that serve as their classrooms here.

As I pull out of the parking lot, Jimi's still singing, "I love you gypsy eyes . . . I love you gypsy eyes," and I am wondering if my two little gypsies will end up as far away from their starting point as I did from mine. I hope that the gravity of this good place will rein in their someday orbits a little closer to home, but the truth is, Matt, I have given them the wandering gene. My people have been restless for a few generations now. We are rarely buried where we were born. Sometimes that's a good thing. Still, this time around, I hope that gene is recessive. Or maybe Grace's influence—her clan almost seventy years on the same piece of ground—will hold sway. *¿Quién sabe?* Anyhow, I hope you and your family are doing well on the eastern end of the road.

Vulture Gulch (April)

Around our house, piñon and juniper elders offer us a little shelter from the wind and weather that often blow in hard from the southwest. Nearby, a little to the south, a line of aspens that follows Crestone Creek down the mountain offers yet another windbreak and harbors warblers and western tanagers during the warmer months, as well as a colony of turkey vultures.

In the mornings the vultures leave their nearby roost, drifting down along the line of aspens then cottonwoods that follow the mountain drainages onto the valley floor, scanning county roads with eye and nose for the latest roadkill. In the evenings, we watch them come home to their perch on the flanks of the Sangres, circling by overhead and spiraling down to their roost in the aspens along Crestone Creek. The arroyo they often seem to follow to and from their roost runs by our house. We call it Vulture Gulch.

One morning almost ten years ago, I enticed my three-year-old daughter into her traveling pack and carry her down the road for a visit with vultures. It was early enough in the morning that few of them had left. As we followed the trail along the creek into a little clearing we saw them overhead, at least twenty vultures, several of them facing toward the sun, their wings outspread and gathering sunlight. "Don't disturb them, Papa," Rosalea said after a minute or two looking up at them in that clearing.

We kept walking. Down the trail, several vultures flew overhead. "Where do you think they're going?" I asked Rosalea.

"They're going to school church," she said.

"Where's that?" I wondered.

"It's way out there," she said, pointing out over the valley. "And it's where your dreams go when you close your eyes."

THE DUCKS (MAY)

I.

I KNOW WHY THE BLACK FOX IS HERE AND WHY IT KEEPS COMING back. This fox smells duck. Our ducks are Rouens, a heavyweight as domesticated ducks go. Think of the Rouen family as gussied-up mallards whose roots are traced back to France, which may explain their unusual breeding behavior. They are not known as prolific egg-layers and we wondered at first if they knew how to make that happen. Throughout the winter, they appeared to be celibate. Then the drake, also known as Sir Francis, or Fronnck as I like to call him, seemed to come into his own. His technique was different; he would mount the hen, also known as Ruida (which means "loud" in Spanish), and push her head under water in their puddle of a pond until she consented, a technique that struck me as decidedly French in a Marquis de Sade sort of way.

I guess he got the deed done. Ruida has been devoted to her nest for the last month, sitting on a dozen or so eggs and becoming increasingly grumpy and aggressive. "She's just a bundle of hormones," says my wife Grace. Ruida no longer emerges from the greenhouse for her daily walk—too busy nesting—but Fronnck still makes his daily pilgrimage to a glass door where he checks up on his reflection, which he apparently perceives as a better-looking date who threatens to come-a-courtin' his hen any day now. So far, Fronnck has kept his competition at bay.

But the black fox, which is really a red fox with dark color variation, may be more than he can handle. These days, Fronnck seems oblivious to the evolving domestic scene, enjoying his solo walks more than he did his coupled outings with a vocal and domineering hen. How quickly he has forgotten her.

II.

When the bodies were found, I took care of the forensics. Who was responsible for the killing and how did it all come down? Grace consoled Caroline, 8, who first discovered the carnage in the greenhouse, and her older sister, Rosalea, 12, who quickly entered into a period of mourning upon hearing the sad news: the ducks—Ruida and Sir Francis the Drake, a.k.a. Fronnck— were dead.

Inside the greenhouse, a noir crime scene if I ever saw one, I considered seeking out a whiskey and a few Pall Malls before proceeding with the investigation. Neither being handy, I proceeded anyway. It was clear from the carnage that Fronnck, since his carcass was gnawed on most heavily, had been the first to meet his sad fate. It was a noble death, I decided, since he had placed himself between the predator and his mate. Ruida, found not far from the nest where she brooded over eggs that never hatched, had no doubt put up a good fight—she was known to be ornery—but she, too, was unable to defend herself. It was all of the grisly scene I had imagined when I first noticed the fox and the coyote casing the joint. And who could blame them? Hunger is the status quo here on the edge. And the ducks were not shy, boldly proclaiming their duckness each morning, which was like announcing the daily menu special for local predators.

But which predator was responsible for their untimely deaths? I searched, without success, for obvious tracks. An interior greenhouse sprinkler may have washed them away. But there was a clear sign in the loft above . . . raccoon scat. And raccoons are known to be good climbers, hanging out in high places where coyote and fox do not tread. They also like to eat ducks.

This was not a quick raid and retreat; we'd tightened up security enough to prevent that. It appeared to have been an inside job and clearly a raccoon had been in residence. That was as much as I could ascertain on the first investigation. Then it was on to the chore of the burial, after which I ventured inside to attend to the bereaved. Caroline was done with grief, proclaiming her desire to watch a movie to take her mind off things. Rosalea, on the other hand, had gone back to bed, burrowing under her covers to fully engage in the grieving process. Having been the first consoler, Grace had moved on to other chores.

Later that day, we gathered and sat in silence, occasionally expressing our thoughts on the sad passing of the ducks. We, the parents, made some remarks about the great chain of being and how some things must die to feed others. Caroline fidgeted, Rosalea listened quietly, and it soon became clear that there was nothing left to say.

BARBIES IN THE
BACKCOUNTRY (JUNE)

THE FIRST TIME I NOTICE THE BARBIES WE ARE A MILE IN FROM THE trailhead. I see them strapped to my youngest daughter's pack as if taken hostage. The Barbies could care less that the load we have carefully packed onto our four-legged porter, a burro named Sabina, is listing to the left and about to flop over. One of the Barbies looks at me, pouty, sassy—*Oh, you're, like, so incompetent*—as I try to shift the load back into place.

When the Barbies make their next appearance, I am secretly happy they have been liberated from my daughter's pack, stripped naked, and set afloat in a very cold mountain stream. The Barbies ride the current, their long, slinky legs goose-bumping off creek-bed cobbles and their carefully coiffed hair trailing like algae behind them. *Get me . . . like . . . out of here.*

How strange this must be for the Barbies . . . to be without their closets full of Barbie clothes, without their pink Corvettes and mini cell phones, hundreds of miles from the nearest mall, headed into a long night with a cold bivouac ahead of them. As if their creek immersion weren't enough, they are now perched in a remnant snowbank near our high-altitude camp, legs akimbo in exotic yoga positions. *Hellowwwwwww . . . we're Barbies not G.I. Joes!*

Poor Barbies. They are now huddled together in a large woolen mitten, having weathered the night dressed only in pink evening gowns. *We didn't . . . like . . . sign up for this.* And yet they are smiling in the morning sun, as if maybe they are proud of their new survival skills.

I am glad that my daughters set the terms when the Barbies come to play, and not the other way around.

QUERENCIA (AN INTERLUDE)

is the space where we are most at home. The sound of
the word takes me to water,

to the river maybe, the nose of a kayak in the heart of a
wave, as it spills over a ledge,

curls back upstream, crests and falls again crests and falls
again and holds the boat

in place, as long as I dip paddle and rudder, keeping to
the sweet spot, where the up

and down currents meet, where there is stillness in
motion, where I am held letting

the sun-slivered water slide by on the glassy edge of a
hole in the river. Dwell as water

on water, blood on blood, surf the heart of it all. You are
here, says *querencia* . . . in this

body, on this river, you are here.

Riding the Tongue (July)

I heard about it all on the way to the river. You had taken a pass on all the gadgets that might win you a few more days to breathe. In your own voiceless way, you told them to keep it real and take you home.

That night, while the summer meteors flashed across the Milky Way, I held you in a prayer, without purpose or destination perhaps, other than the moment it made. Clear. Your eyes. Deep like the trout-finning pools in the river below camp.

Next morning, I forgot about you. It was the light playing on the water. You know how it is. You paddle through it, mesmerized by the shimmer of it all, riding its shine like dragonflies delirious in their coupling flight.

We camped above the big rapid that night, the one we feared the most. I was listening to the crickets—those that drone and those that chant—when a screech owl flew out of its own silhouette and took its shadow downstream.

By then you were at home, maybe in a bed beside the window, looking out on the mountain whose thermals you knew well. Below our camp, the owl perched above that glassy slant of water at the top of the rapid—the tongue that always says "over

here"—and the current that would glide us, come morning,
beyond the ledge where the river disappears.

THE SHIFT (AUGUST)

IT IS THE THIRD WEEK IN AUGUST. FOR THE LAST TWO MONTHS, THE sunrise has been sliding south on the eastern horizon, but today is the first day I've noticed. Today the morning light seems softer. The aspens and cottonwoods throw out a little more shade during the day. The heat and glare at high noon are no longer so oppressive. The mosquitos are gone. A subtle chill rides in on the evening breeze. It is lovely, but it is bittersweet.

Today I feel the shift in a spare moment. It is quiet except for the bees buzzing in the hive outside my window. The sunflowers Grace planted in June, now tall and gangly, swoon in a slight breeze. Whatever wind there is up high isn't strong enough to nudge some lazy clouds over the Sangres. I haven't finished unpacking from a long road trip, the last one of the season. The camper on the back of the truck needs to come off, but instead I grab a cold beer and watch baseball.

It is still summer and it isn't. It is because the walking rains still saunter across the valley, shedding a double rainbow on the mountain this evening, reminding me of a similar time, fifteen years ago, when we arrived here—young parents with a new baby—wondering if this place would welcome us. It is still summer because there is enough time left for the Bucs to recover their groove and snag a wild-card ticket into the post-season.

It is no longer summer because I have overindulged at too many barbecues. We have put thousands of miles on the Chevy. I have put the river gear away. And the call of the teaching vocation demands more of my time.

But there are openings for recollection in this shifting season, for gathering a few summer moments to carry into this next turn of the wheel, like that solstice-day run on the Arkansas, dipping the oars into the shining whitewater I hadn't seen since the old guiding days thirty-some years ago, listening to the laughter of my two daughters, now old enough to enjoy each new wave together.

Two days ago, I heard that Michael, an old pal here, had died after a short bout with cancer. I knew he was sick and I had been thinking about him on the long road home. Lately I've been thinking about all the good cheer and conversation we shared. I miss him. Rest in peace, amigo.

Tonight the crickets are singing. Cygnus the Swan will glide further west across the night sky, leaving celestial space for the rising stars of autumn. And it occurs to me that happiness comes and goes like the constellations, but joy stays with us like Polaris, the North Star. It is the residual shine from savored moments with friends and loved ones that we carry into the longer nights ahead.

THE PIÑON (SEPTEMBER)

THE PIÑON PINE IS A GIVING TREE. THE JAYS HAVE KNOWN THIS FOR a long time. Maybe they were the first to find out. Now they move in raucous flocks, boisterous as flying frat parties, gathering and caching piñon nuts in tree crevices and under pine needles for the season of shorter days ahead. And as the jays pay it forward by finding new ground for these heavy, wingless seeds, the trees nod their thanks in a light wind out of the southwest.

It is as if that same wind carried the news from the jays to some hunter-gatherer a long time ago—harvest these nuts, crack them open, and eat. And the word was carried down through the ages to the ancestors of the Paiute and the Shoshone in the Great Basin, and those of the Hopis and the Utes and later the Navajo on the Colorado Plateau, and the Pueblos along the Rio Grande. And the Pueblos and Utes told the Spanish. And the Spanish told their children, who told their children, and so on. And now the word spreads from a brother to a sister to a cousin to a father, through all the old family trees here in the San Luis Valley, until everyone knows that there are no nuts in Tres Piedras this year, but the trees in Crestone are heavy with gifts.

And so families of gleaners from all over the valley arrive here on my street every Saturday morning. "Word gets around," says one of the gleaners. "We don't need Facebook." And this past

Saturday we join in the harvest. My wife, my daughters, and our neighbor sit in the October sun, on a pine-needled south-facing slope, under one of the piñons here that is old enough to have fed pilgrims along the Old Spanish Trail a few hundred years ago. And the sun warms us as we run our hands through the pine needles, sifting out the good nuts. And we fill our jars, and fill each other's jars, as the piñon jays screech by overhead, spreading the good news. It is a kind of communion.

And down the street, there are other families, some from as far away as New Mexico. Children do their gathering along the ground, while their mothers and fathers and grandparents shake piñon branches, the nuts raining down on tarps they have spread out under the trees. One old grandma catches them in an inverted umbrella. And there is laughter and there are smiles. And there is time to be with one another on a beautiful September morning.

Later in the day, we are done, but the other families carry on. Down the road, I find one family finishing lunch. The sun is higher now and I wonder if they would rather spend the afternoon harvesting around the big piñons behind our house, where there is more shade and more bounty than we can handle. *Yes*, they say, packing up their tailgate lunch—tortillas, Cheese Whiz, green chiles, and salsa—*we'll follow you*. And so we drive together back up to our house. And they get out with their tarps and empty Maxwell House coffee cans. The mom tells me that she is from Chama. Her children are silently polite. And her father, an older man from Center, asks me if I like potatoes. And I say sure. And he says he will be back in a week and bring me some.

THE BIG CAT (OCTOBER)

EASTBOUND CLOUDS STALL OUT OVER THE HIGH PEAKS OF THE SAN-gres. Others, low and gray, drape the big valley sky to the west. It is a restless season. The bears are on the move—such a fierce hunger before the big sleep—and the rose hips are ripe. A bull elk climbs slopes so thick with piñon and juniper, it's hard to guide his big rack through the branches. He is moving away from last night's smoke, the hunter's fire. And he is moving away from Grace and me who are walking and talking quietly on the trail below him, watching our white dog nosing through a pile of old cow bones.

We follow the cottonwood trees that line the stream, wondering how far it will flow before the veins of the aquifer take it underground. Maybe they already have. Whether it is water or a slight wind we are hearing, it is a thin sound in a wide silence, a silence instantly shattered by the white dog who rips through the brush and into the clearing, followed by a cougar, one flying stride behind him and closing in fast.

HOLYSHHHEEEOWWWWW, I yell, loud as I can from my middle-aged lungs. The cougar, dead still now, turns his gaze to us. The white dog, having left the scene, barks with great bravado. Look tall, I'm thinking as the cougar hisses between big teeth and stares us down. Look very tall. And he stares us down some more. And he lets loose this weird gurgling groan. Grace talks to the cougar—"Hello, mootieekins"—as if it's one of her house cats, and it angles in toward us.

"Don't do that," I whisper, "we're cat chow here." Look taller. Then again, maybe she's right. Maybe her voice soothes the big cat, who veers off now into the willows, looking over its shoulder. As we slowly back away, I grab a rock, as if I could fend off the charge of a full-grown cougar. Meantime, the white dog, who is beyond the trees and in the clear, catches the odor of something dead farther out in the valley and runs toward it. He has already forgotten what just went down.

We won't.

THE FREE BOX
(NOVEMBER)

THE FREE BOX IS NO LONGER JUST A BOX. NOW IT'S A SHED ON THE edge of town, roof rimmed with wind-worn Tibetan prayer flags, an old mattress leaning up against the front wall spray-painted with the words "No dumping." The contributions I bring include some lightly used fairy wings—still the rage in preschool fashion—and bench seat covers from Autozone which won't add to the clutter for long. But I worry about the mini John Deere tractor/sprinkler taking up space, since it's November and a big winter front will soon bury the few lawns in town.

Having put my unwanted stuff on display, I scan through pairs of shoes ready to step off their shelves—moccasins, Birkenstocks, three-pin cross-country ski boots; clothes that mingle in overflowing plywood bins—tie-dyed "Yes We Can" T-shirt, an old raccoon hat, blue gym shorts, and shiny Denver Bronco warm-up pants; a few well-worn titles on the bookshelf—*The Mars and Venus Diet & Exercise Solution, Winning Sweepstakes: A Proven Guide, Women Coming of Age* by Jane Fonda; odds and ends in the weekend warrior handyman's emporium—an unused tube of caulk, a jar full of 16-penny nails, a hammer head (no handle) and a hacksaw (no blade); and in the toy box, an old Slinky, a squirt gun, and a bald doll missing an eye. Just as I am about to leave, a neo-Rastafarian couple with identical dreadlocks enters the shed for a quick browse, and the guy walks off with the John Deere tractor/sprinkler. You never know.

Then I notice an old travel trunk in a corner of the shed. The label on the lid reads, "community memory exchange." As soon as I open it, I am clouded in the smells of patchouli, burning sage, reefer smoke, the incense-filled memories belonging to my neighbors. In a quickly deepening delirium, I try to close the lid, but the feedback from a cranked-up Stratocaster and the roar of a hundred Harleys blasts it open again. Next Hare Krishna, Hare Rama, and an orange-robed baldy with a free-dinner invite. And now a drum circle at the 1973 gathering of the Rainbow Family in Nevada. And then someone tasting a strawberry with Werner Erhard at an EST seminar in 1975. Whoa. Enough. I slam the lid shut. No more memories for me, thanks. I can barely manage the ones I have.

BLACK ICE (DECEMBER)

THIS MOUNTAIN LAKE LIVES IN SHADOW. THE SUN IS A ROUNDER . . .
stays away longer each night, and sleeps it off behind the ridge
during the day. The winds come down off the mountain, sweep-
ing skiffs of snow across the ice. A father pulls on his skates, so
much easier now with plastic and Velcro than it once was with
leather and lace. He tests the freeze, first around the edges—a
few feet thick—then out in the middle—clear and so deep, he
can't tell where the ice leaves off and the black water begins.
He skates as fast as he can, grateful this sprint is his own—no
whistles, no coach. He slides one blade in front of the other,
leans into a wide rink turn, and carves two thin white lines that
follow him out to the edge of the lake where his daughter, still
wobbly in her new pink skates, glides toward him. He takes her
hands in his and skates backwards, looking over his shoulder for
stones frozen in the ice, then back at his daughter who, steady
now, sees only what lies ahead.

IV.

THE BIG EMPTY

*"We walk aware of what is far and close.
Here distance is familiar as a friend."*

—Theodore Roethke

*"Whole symphonies . . .
live between
here and a distant whatever we look at."*

—Richard Hugo

WHERE I AM

I COULD TELL YOU TO TURN EAST ONTO THE COUNTY ROAD JUST SOUTH
of Moffat. I could give you a street address and a phone number.
I could tell you we are the last house on the left before you hit
Crestone Creek. I might suggest that you look for the vultures
circling in the end-of-day sky just west of the Sangre de Cristos.
Maybe I'll be there.

But a part of me stays further south beyond the trailhead where
the wildlife refuge begins. Check the creekbed that threads out
into the valley. Look for a western tanager perched on a cottonwood branch, or a mountain bluebird that carries the sky across
a hidden meadow where there is always a pool of dappled light
and it is so quiet you can hear the dead sing.

Here the wind has scoured out the sand, except for a ridge held
in place by two old ponderosas, down which a mothering elk and
her two calves descend at dusk for a drink from the creek. Later,
the constellations ride by overhead—Cygnus, Delphinus, Aquila.

Even they are transient.

I listen for whatever it is that stays.

LETTER TO A YOUNG SWAMPER

It is the summer of 1976, you have just turned twenty, and you have landed your dream job. You arrive at Lee's Ferry in a U-Haul truck full of vintage World War II rubber. And as you are blowing shop-vac air into two long outrigger tubes soon to be strapped to an aluminum frame which is itself strapped to an elongated rubber donut that holds this whole scow together, you realize that, yes, this boat is a pig compared to those powered only by muscle and oars, but at least you won't have to run that triple-rig on the beach beside you, where an old and leathery L.A. woman in a faux leopard-skin bathing suit orders around her harem of boatmen who are inflating not one, but three big rafts lashed side-by-side. Your boat is a thirty-three-foot barge, sleek in comparison, which will ferry you, the head boatman, fifteen passengers, and a week's worth of groceries to feed them, cases upon cases of cold Coors, and a Porta Potty, also known as the groover, down the Colorado to Lake Mead. You will spend ten days riding in the back of the barge, savoring the changing palette of limestones, sandstones, and shales that seduced you after that first trip down the river years ago. And you will breathe in the fumes of a Mercury outboard, admiring the skills of your ex-Amy-boss boatman who pirouettes your barge around massive boils of whitewater foaming up out of huge river craters that could swallow a mobile home without spitting out the evidence. Clearly, the river says, you do not know your ass from a hole in the ground.

Now you have a few trips under your belt and you are a seasoned swamper, which is really just another way of saying Big Ditch longshoreman (without union pay) who occasionally runs a rapid or two, but who mostly ferries stuff from boat to beach and beach to boat, bushwhacks through tamarisk thickets looking for a weedy trunk thick enough for a bow-line tie-down, pumps air back into the neoprene pig in the cool canyon morning, and digs holes underneath the groover. This is not glamorous work, but at least you know the difference between your ass and *this* hole in the ground.

Soon you are beginning to dream the river at night. It helps that you sleep out on the boat—your barge is good for that—although you do wake from time to time imagining you have come unmoored and are headed downriver to Crystal. You jump up and check the rope and thank Tao you are still tethered to solid ground, so you climb back into your bag. And before it is time to get up and kindle a fire for morning coffee, you savor a few dreamtime lines—gracefully steering your rig down through the rocky-fanged gap at the head of Horn Creek or gliding down one tongue of glassy green water after another into the shining good-time waves of the rapids you have come to know as the gems—Turquoise, Sapphire, Ruby. And later, during your waking hours, you accept a pinch of Copenhagen from your boot-camp boss after Havasu, which will help you stay awake as you motor the long stretch of post-lunch flat water down to Lava Falls, where you go up on the ledge above the river, and stare into the great frothing mess of the BIG ONE until the columnar lines in the basalt across the river seem to be melting in the sun. Your mind wanders while your boot-camp boss describes his line through Lava. And then he says, "Well, are you ready to run it?" And you hope like hell, as you walk back down that rocky trail toward your nervous passengers, that at least for a few choice river moments, you *will* know your ass from a hole in the ground.

It has been five years or so since you abandoned your motor-rig apprenticeship, and you have been rowing smaller boats down mountain rivers in Colorado and Utah. And now the time has come for your first private trip back down through your old swamping grounds. You row a thirteen-foot Miwok down the river you once knew only on the big rigs and you feel small, but not so small that you don't chase a line between two huge holes, which erupt into a cauldron of foam that sends you ass-over-tea-kettle faster than you can say Sockdolager, and you are gasping for breath under the bottom of your boat for the first time. But the rest of the trip goes well, and then you run into your old outfit at Diamond Creek and there's your boot-camp boss loading rubber into a U-Haul and you remember your first run through Lava and how he raised a beer to you out on the barge after dinner that night. On the road out of Diamond Creek, you also recall the terror of treading water under your boat after that run gone wrong in "Sock," but even a bad line will likely get you farther down the river . . . a little closer, if you're paying attention, to knowing your ass from a hole in the ground.

A few decades later, you will drive your daughter up the old road past Marble Canyon and the turnoff to Lee's Ferry, past Vermilion Cliffs where your boot-camp river boss once lived and maybe still does and where there used to be a great little tavern for boatmen between trips, where you vaguely recall chasing a girl or two, where you once listened in awe, albeit from a few bar stools down—you were only a young punk swamper after all—to your river elders telling tales . . . Jimmy Hall, like one of Huckleberry's riverboat gamblers, bragging about running the table with a shovel-handle pool cue, or that bighearted soul you knew only as Whale recalling a close-call-of-a-run through Crystal. You will think of them as you drive up the switchbacks of the Kaibab, which you once rode down on the roof of the company U-Haul, and then you will forget about them as you follow the dirt road out to the North Rim. And as you look down from Point Sublime, through the big empty toward that thread of a river, which you have not been on for over thirty years, you will wonder, since you're now approaching sixty, if you will ever row your daughters down that river. Sure you will. You must. You have to show them the canyon from the river up, this place where maybe you learned the difference between your ass and a hole in the ground. Where at least you know now, they really aren't that far apart.

WATERSHED

Where you begin   is   never the beginning   you always
below the high snowfields   not the beginning either   and
above the ocean   never stays   where you end is a different
question   the sign at the cemetery says burial permits required:
please check in before you check out   i am of this place now
but i won't be left in its ground   drifters are water dwellers   But say my ashes end up in Crestone Creek and they go
under   i mean we live on a rift the Rio Grande Rift   and it's
a big deep fault   the water goes down and down through the
blue clay   and stays there a long time   i mean a long time   i
mean the water goes down in those dark fissures to a time before
dinosaurs and ice age   so when my daughter says where does
the creek go i say it goes to the ocean   and maybe it does and
maybe it doesn't   i mean there's a lot of water down there not
going anywhere anytime soon   this water, these rocks take
their own fine time   they   take   their   own   fine   time.

POSTCARD TO THE PADRE

I CAN'T FIND THE SCREW-TOP OF THE SILVER FLASK YOU LEFT ME, which I especially regret because I have yet to enjoy its liquid warmth on the mountain as you did after days on the shining Yukon ice, having crossed the snow bridges that straddled the yawning blue deepdown. This flask curves around my thigh as it did yours. We were both blessed with strong legs to carry us to high places, but I am not as surefooted. You took communion, pouring the rose-colored wine into the goblet you placed on a slab of granite in the Sierras. You saw the backlit pines as angels. You knew Elijah's still, small voice in the peaks above those Canadian crevasses. In the high-noon flat light of this half-life plus, snow covers the ice ahead and I'll be damned if I can read the contours.

A XEROPHILE'S CONFESSION

XEROPHILE (from Greek xeros, meaning 'dry', and philos loving); "a plant or animal that is adapted for growing or living in dry conditions."

--Collins Dictionary

THEY WILL GIVE ME ALL THEIR BOOKS, FINGERS RUNNING THROUGH the texts: This is it—holy, holy—this is it. But those thisses are not it. God is he; no not he, she . . . but no pronoun will hold that center, unless maybe Thou?

A woman in the supermarket says Jesus led her to a cheaper turkey—*attention all born-again shoppers*—and for a moment I envy her mainline intimacy. Maybe I just wasn't listening.

Those who fret over the "G" word will say the universe willed it. I say the universe has better things to do. They tell me you create your own reality. I say, sorry, the weather arrives on its own.

So I am led again to the holiness of zero, the righteousness of nada, nada, nada. But what will hold me when I fall? Is there a thermal there, but not there? And if there is, what of the ground that shaped it?

NOWHERE CAFÉ

SOON IT COMES BACK TO YOU, THIS LONELIEST ROAD RHYTHM FOL-
lowing a Nevada moon out of the troughs of the great ghost
waves, beyond the piñon summits, and down the far side of
range after range, where there is always another valley—
greasewood, saltbush, alkali—and one less radio station.

It takes longer to get nowhere than it used to. You see what
looks like the glow of a small town over the rise, and you
wonder if it's real or maybe some coffeed-up apparition, like
that hitchhiking shadow a few miles back. You round a bend
and there lies a dying town.

Home of the Nowhere Café.

Go slow. The café is easy to pass—they shut the lights off
years ago. Out back, where the truckers used to park, you
follow a road running south between the ranges they call
Shoshone and Toiyabe. So close to nowhere now, you've
gone giddy. You hear yourself chanting: *Shoshone, Toiyabe,
Shoshone, Toiyabe.*

You take the first two-track turn, follow it out to the end,
shut the lights off, shut the engine off, and sit tight till it
stops ticking. Then you walk out over this desert hardpan,

wait for the first falling star, and you hear . . . nothing . . . not even a lick of wind. Finally, you are nowhere.

And you say the only words you have left to say: Empty me . . . that I might be whole again.

ACKNOWLEDGMENTS

The following pieces were originally published in journals and anthologies: "Night Ride in the Red Desert" and "True News from a Small-Town Beat" (*New Poets of the American West,* Many Voices Press); "Backbumper Gospel" (*Fruita Pulp*); "Summer Crossing" (*The Best of Friends, Volume 1,* Kimo Press); "Riding the Tongue" (*Mountain Gazette*); "A Xerophile's Confession" (*Desert Call*); "Letter to Jack Kerouac after Rereading *On the Road*" and "Nowhere Café" (*Storied Wheels,* Somos Publications); "Letter to a Young Swamper" (*Boatman's Quarterly*); "Watershed" and "Querencia" (*Sage Green Journal*).

Earlier versions of the following originally appeared in "Dispatches from the Edge," a bimonthly column in *Colorado Central Magazine*: "Letter from the Mother Road"; "Rodeo Weekend, Duchesne, Utah"; "Letter to Jack Kerouac after Rereading *On the Road*"; "Letter from the Side of the Mountain"; "The Ranger and the Porcupine"; "Christmas in Yellowstone"; "Gringo's Lingo for a Night on the Town"; "Great Divide Lonely Hearts Club"; "Barbies in the Backcountry"; "Bats"; "Fireflies."

About the Author

PETER ANDERSON WAS THE BENNETT FELLOW WRITER-IN-RESIDENCE at Phillips Exeter Academy for the 2015-16 school year. His most recent books include *Heading Home: Field Notes* (Conundrum Press, 2017), a collection of flash prose and prose poems exploring rural life and the modern day eccentricities of the American West; *Going Down Grand: Poems from the Canyon* (Lithic Press, 2015), an anthology of Grand Canyon poems edited with Rick Kempa, which was nominated for a Colorado Book Award; and *First Church of the Higher Elevations: Mountains, Prayer and Presence* (Conundrum Press, 2015), a collection of essays on wildness, mountain places, and the life of the spirit. Peter teaches writing at Adams State University in Alamosa, Colorado and lives with his family on the western slope of the Sangre de Cristo Range.